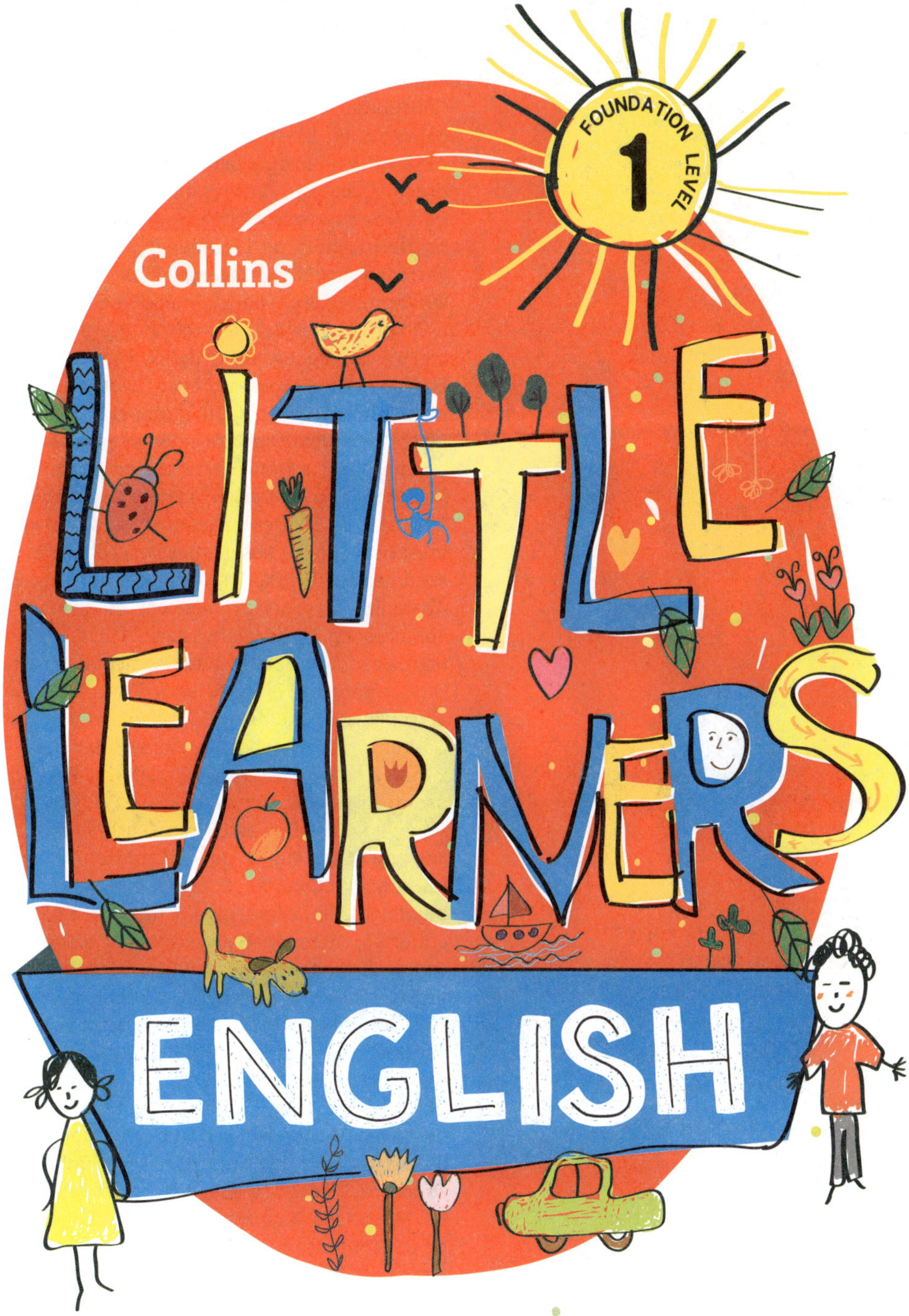

SERIES EDITOR: RANI T.

Published by Collins Learning
A division of HarperCollins*Publishers*
India Private Limited

HarperCollins Publishers
Building No. 10, Tower A, 4th Floor, DLF Cyber City, Gurugram, Haryana 122002, India

1 London Bridge Street, London, SE1 9GF, United Kingdom

2 Bloor Street East, Toronto, Ontario M4W 1A8, Canada

Lvl 13, 201 Elizabeth Street (PO Box A565, NSW, 1235), Sydney NSW 2000, Australia

195 Broadway, New York, NY 10007, USA

Browse the complete Collins catalogue at www.collins.in
For any queries/feedback, please write to us at **SCHOOLSUPPORT@harpercollins.co.in** or call us on **0124-4894800**.

First published in 2020

Reprint: 10 9 8 7 6 5 4 3 2 1

ISBN: 978-935357-030-9

Artwork and layout by
Qualibre Creatives Pvt. Ltd.

Printed and bound by
MicroPrints India, New Delhi

Acknowledgements

Cover: HarperCollins*Publishers*India

Title Page: HarperCollins*Publishers*India

Prelim Pages: radenmas, denkcreative, nonohana, graphic-bee

Inside: pg 8,9: eliflamra, nyamol, **pg 10:** eliflamra, nyamol, Redlio Designs, blueringmedia, LeeDaniels, nataka, Tomacco, aldo_nat; **pg 11:** artbesouro, neyro2008, Iv__design, ONYXprj, Olga_Mallari, TopVectors, Tetiana Lazunova, graphxarts, ChrisGorgio, -ELIKA-, Zhenyakot, Vectorpower, VectorUp, filo, colematt; **pg 12:** eliflamra, **pg 13:** nyamol, eliflamra, viyadaistock, Abscent84, StudioBarcelona; **pg 14:** nyamol, **pg 15:** graphic-bee, draco77, digigops, Vasilyevalara, Redlio Designs; **pg 16:** nyamol, **pg 17:** Sudowoodo, ONYXprj, nyamol, Yulia Ogneva, denis_pc; **pg 18:** colematt; **pg 19:** blueringmedia, denis_pc, sonicken, hermandesign2015, AndreyMakurin; **pg 20:** nyamol, graphic-bee, ONYXprj, sonicken; **pg 21:** StudioBarcelona, graphic-bee, Abscent84, ONYXprj, AndreyMakurin, hermandesign2015, draco77, denis_pc, mejnak, StudioBarcelona; **pg 22:** nyamol, **pg 23:** Bigmouse108, krishna pethani, kolotuschenko, nyamol, Sky_melody; **pg 24:** abstractdesignlabs; **pg 25:** skalapendra, stevezmina1, nyamol, pleshko74, KRIKUN;**pg 26:** colematt; pg 27: graphic-bee,colematt, bandian1122, ikryannikovgmailcom, Dreamcreation; **pg 28:** pleshko74, **pg 29:** DesignTogether, Sudowoodo, LeeDaniels, Tomacco; **pg 30:** DesignTogether, kolotuschenko, graphic-bee, pleshko74; **pg 31:** krishna pethani, colematt, LeeDaniels, nyamol, skalapendra, ONYXprj, graphic-bee, stevezmina1, skalapendra, Abscent84, ikryannikovgmailcom, bandian1122, neyro2008, Tomacco; **pg 34:** hermandesign2015, **pg 35:** Tomacco, nyamol, helloween, neyro2008, blueringmedia, miniature; **pg 36:** Dualororua; **pg 37:** MariaTkach, Pavel Naumov, FARBAI, aqabiz, vectorikart; **pg 39 :** Usagi-D, **pg 39:** andegro4ka, artbesouro, Godruma, vladwel; **pg 40:** AndreyMakurin; **pg 41:** andegro4ka, Ennessy, soyonillust, Alliya23; **pg 42:** ARNICAart, ARNICAart, asantosg, aqabiz, Nosyrevy, ksenya_savva, Rocksana, Mikhaylova_ Anna; **pg 43:** helloween, MariaTkach, Alliya23, colematt; **pg 44,45:** xxxx; **pg 46:** colematt; **pg 47:** PeterHermesFurian, Amin Yusifov, kbeis; **pg 48:** Caterina_K; **pg 49:** colematt, eliflamra, seamartini, blueringmedia, 2Xena; **pg 50:** nyamol; **pg 51:** ChrisGorgio, eliflamra, Aleksangel, drogatnev; **pg 52:** AndreyMakurin; **pg 53:** Octopus182, hermandesign2015, d1sk, luplupme, seamartini; **pg 54:** Ennessy, Amin Yusifov, schlol, colematt, blueringmedia, ChrisGorgio, eliflamra, Godruma, Octopus182, luplupme; **pg 55:** eliflamra, hermandesign2015, PeterHermesFurian, soyonillust, Octopus182, seamartini, Ennessy, luplupme, blueringmedia; **pg 56:** Dualororua; **pg 57:** yayayoyo, Toltemara, Tetiana Lazunova, fineye; **pg 58:** bandian1122; **pg 59:** graphic-bee, Photoplotnikov, hermandesign2015, TatianaKulikova, Bullet_Chained; **pg 61:** VladSt, FaberrInk, Tigatelu, pleshko74, seamartini; **pg 62:** AndreyMakurin; **pg 63:** MicrovOne, Thomas Lydell, colematt, adekvat; **pg 63:** Tigatelu; **pg 65:** TopVectors, -ELIKA-, siiixth, eliflamra, aqabiz; **pg 66:** Tetiana Lazunova, hermandesign2015, Tigatelu, adekvat, -ELIKA-; **pg 67:** Muhammad Desta Laksana, **pg 68:** Anaboo; **pg 69:** luplupme, setory, S-S-S, klerik78; **pg 71:** Vectorpower, Vaibhav Designer, bennyb, brgfx; **pg72:** Vector Tradition; **pg 73:** IconicBestiary, Alxyzt, filo, vectorsmarket; **pg74:** Muhammad Desta Laksana; **pg 75:** TopVectors, blueringmedia, Weenee, Ksenica; **pg 76:** colematt; **pg 77:** ryccio, colematt, eduardrobert, o-che, siridhata; **pg 78:** Nayanba Jadeja, Nosyrevy; **pg 80:** BerSonnE; **pg 83:** nyamol, graphic-bee, denis_pc, kolotuschenko, skalapendra, helloween, neyro2008, MariaTkach, andegro4ka, kbeis, blueringmedia, drogatnev; **pg 85;** Pavel Naumov, Toltemara, Bullet_Chained, FaberrInk, -ELIKA-, luplupme, Vectorpower, filo, blueringmedia, ryccio.

Preface

Collins Little Learners, comprising 20 books in all, provides graded, age-appropriate learning opportunities targeting holistic skill development for children in the age group of 3 years to 6 years. Spread across three levels, the series spans **English**, **Maths**, **General Awareness**, **Art and Craft** and **Hindi**. The series comes bundled with a **workbook** for English and a book of **rhymes and stories** for each level. The books use a combination of hands-on activities, frequent recapitulation and child-friendly artwork to facilitate learning.

The early years are the most significant years for growth, development and learning. During this period, children need adequate opportunities for stimulating experiences as these favourably affect various learning abilities. Learning experiences, when chosen and planned properly, fuel the innate curiosity of children, and stimulate their thought processes.

Learning and Development During the Early Years

The goal of learning during the early years is to enhance the all-round development of personality and to inculcate healthy attitudes, life skills and good values. Creative play, well thought-out games and developmentally appropriate activities help children develop the necessary skills to achieve these goals. The skills that children need to acquire can broadly be categorized as:

Motor: Motor skills pertain not only to gross motor activities like walking and jumping but also include fine motor activities like the ability to hold a pencil and write. The development of motor skills is facilitated through several graded activities.

Personal, Social and Emotional: Personal, social and emotional development, necessary for the overall personality development of children, is achieved using a combination of hands-on activities, role plays, and thought-provoking stories and rhymes.

Linguistic: The ability to listen, speak, read and write is critical to success in formal learning environments.

Mathematical: The development of mathematical ideas and concepts is important at this stage since children will continue to build on this learning for most of their years of schooling.

Knowledge and Understanding of the World: This is achieved through activities that enable children to explore their surroundings at home and in the school, and interact with the people that they see around them.

Health and Safety: The idea of health and safety is introduced through activities, stories and re-telling of real-life experiences to encourage children to focus on health and well-being.

Creative: Creative skills are developed through a host of activities involving art, craft, painting, roleplays, etc.

Logical and Rational Thinking: Activities that involve simple puzzles, pattern-completion and visual discrimination help children to develop logical and rational thinking skills.

The Collins Little Learners Teacher Support Materials

The series includes extensive teacher support in the form of:

Teacher's Resource Books: Comprises stories, activity banks, classroom management and assessment guidelines

Multimedia eBook: Consists of animations, audio, video, slide shows, and interactive exercises

Print-ready Worksheets: Additional worksheets for practice and reinforcement, present in the digital support

Digital Flashcards: Flashcards with embedded sounds and animations for letter formation and letter-sound association

Animations and Songs: Animated stories and rhymes set to tune

Interactive Games: Interactivities to reinforce concepts in a fun and engaging manner

A note on the activity banks (included in the Teacher's Manuals)

The activity banks comprise hands-on activities that will help children develop the requisite skills to attain age-appropriate learning goals. In keeping with Howard Gardener's theory of multiple intelligences, the activity banks include options and variations that enable teachers to provide a planned cycle of experiences and opportunities, which foster each type of intelligence, to every child in their classrooms. The activity banks equip teachers to use the strengths of children as a means of complementing their less developed areas by valuing and nurturing the inherent abilities of the children.

Contents

Walkthrough

Both upper case and lower case letters shown with pattern tracing to facilitate identification and recognition.

Exercise to reinforce letter-sound association and support vocabulary development

Pattern tracing included for fine motor development

Two-page spreads used to introduce letters. The emphasis is on improving identification of letters and developing letter–sound association through a variety of exercises. The teacher's manual includes stories, which can be used to accomplish these goals.

Varied revision activity formats to ensure holistic skill development

Simple revision exercises such as this help to reinforce concepts

Revision activities such as these enable teachers to assess level of learning and recall without a formal assessment

Simple board game for revision of letter sounds, formations, etc. in small groups to facilitate revision and reinforcement of concepts.

Letters of the Alphabet

Say the letter names. Trace the letters with your fingers.

Mm Nn Oo
Pp Qq Rr
Ss Tt Uu
Vv Ww Xx
Yy Zz

Listen and Sing

Touch the pictures. Sing the song.

A is for ant, B is for ball
C is for cow, D is for doll
E is for elephant, big and strong
She has a trunk, oh so long!

F is for fox, G is for goose
H is for horse, I is for igloo
J is for juice, sweet and yummy
How happy it makes my tummy!

K is for king, L is for light
M is for monkey, N is for night
O is for orange, P for penguin white and black
See how he walks, like this and that!

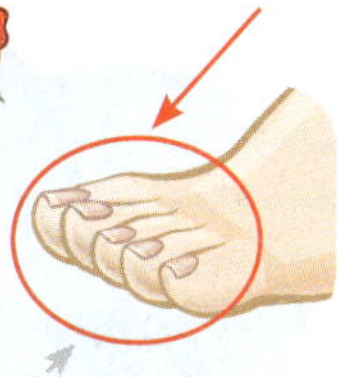

Q is for queen, R is for rose
S is for sun, T is for toes
U is for umbrella, colourful and bright
It keeps me dry in rain alright!

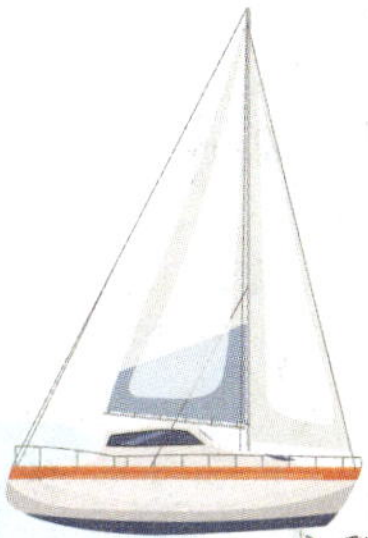

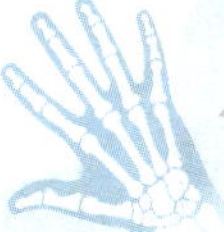

V is for van, W is for watch
X is for x-ray, Y is for yacht
Z is for zebra, dark and light
See how he walks, right-left-right!

Hello Letter Aa

alligator

Touch the pictures. Name them.

ant

alligator

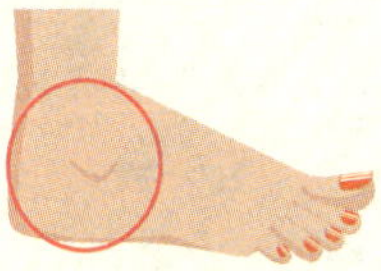

ankle

axe

apple

Trace with your finger.

Hello Letter Bb

Touch the pictures. Name them.

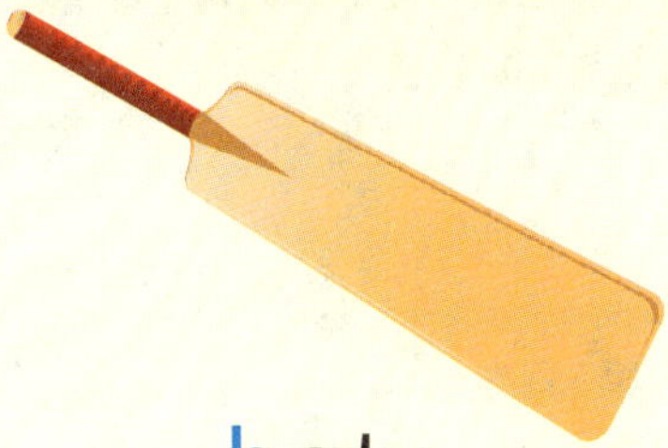

bat

boy

bag

butter

ball

Trace with your finger.

Hello Letter Cc

Touch the pictures. Name them.

cup

cow

cap

cot

cat

Trace with your finger.

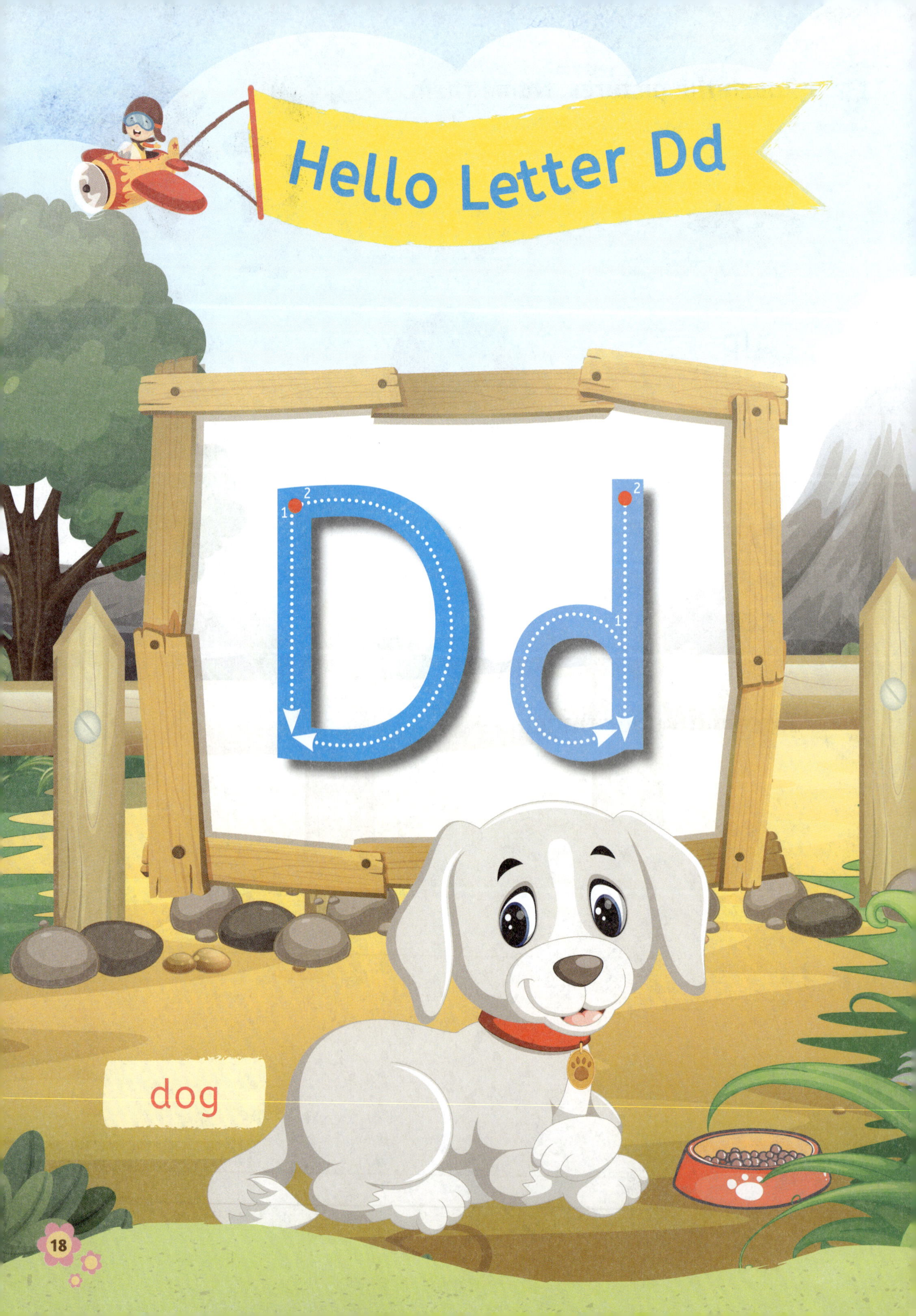
Hello Letter Dd
Dd
dog

Touch the pictures. Name them.

doll

duck

deer

dog

den

Trace with your finger.

I Know Letters Aa–Dd

Match the capital letters to the small letters.

A	d
B	a
C	b
D	c

Name the pictures. Thumbprint the letter it begins with.

a b

c b

d c

d a

Cross (×) the odd one out.

 A 

 B 

 C 

 D 

Match the picture to the letter it begins with.

 • A

 • B

 • C

 • D

Hello Letter Ee

Touch the pictures. Name them.

engine

egg

envelope

elephant

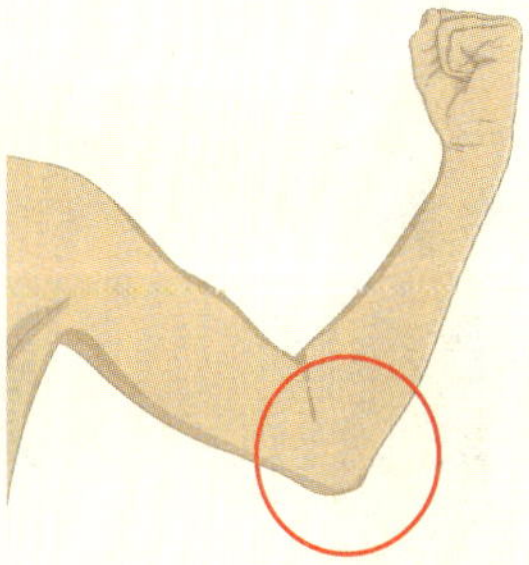

elbow

Trace with your finger.

Hello Letter Ff

Touch the pictures. Name them.

fan

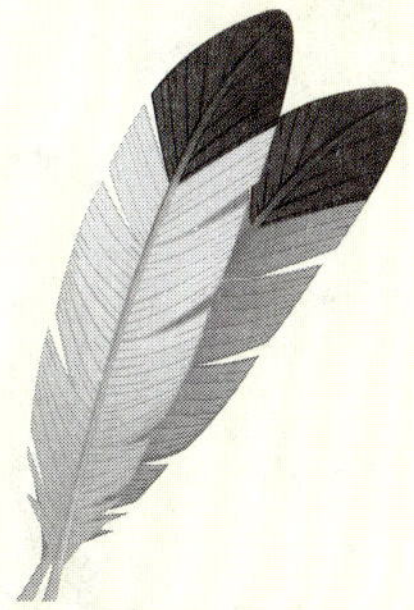

feather

frog

fish

fig

Trace with your finger.

Hello Letter Gg

Touch the pictures. Name them.

girl

goat

grass

gate

gorilla

Trace with your finger.

Hello Letter Hh

Hh

hippopotamus

Touch the pictures. Name them.

hen

house

hat

horse

hut

Trace with your finger.

I Know Letters Ee-Hh

Match the capital letters to the small letters.

E	h
F	e
G	f
H	g

Paste matching letter stickers with each picture.

Match the picture to the letter it begins with.

H

F

G

E

Cross (×) the odd one out.

E

F

G

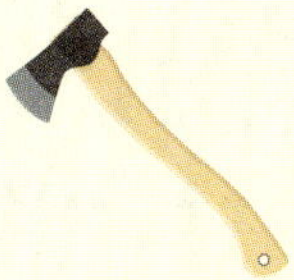  

H

Fun Time

Spot the 6 differences between the two pictures.

Look at the picture. Talk about it.

Hello Letter Ii

Touch the pictures. Name them.

igloo

insect

ink

ill

India

Trace with your finger.

Hello Letter Jj

J j

jaguar

Touch the pictures. Name them.

jug

jam

jar

joker

jacket

Trace with your finger.

Hello Letter Kk

Kk

kangaroo

Touch the pictures. Name them.

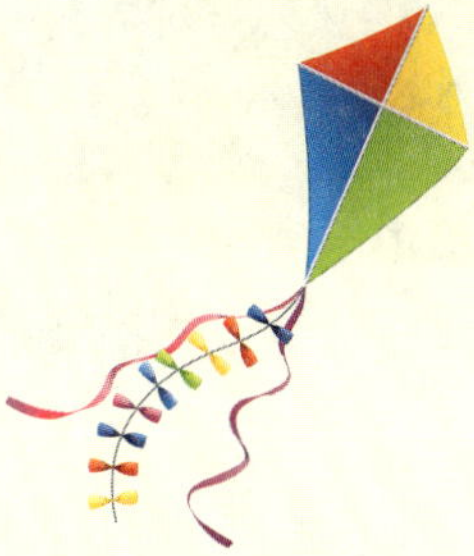

kite

kangaroo

king

kettle

key

Trace with your finger.

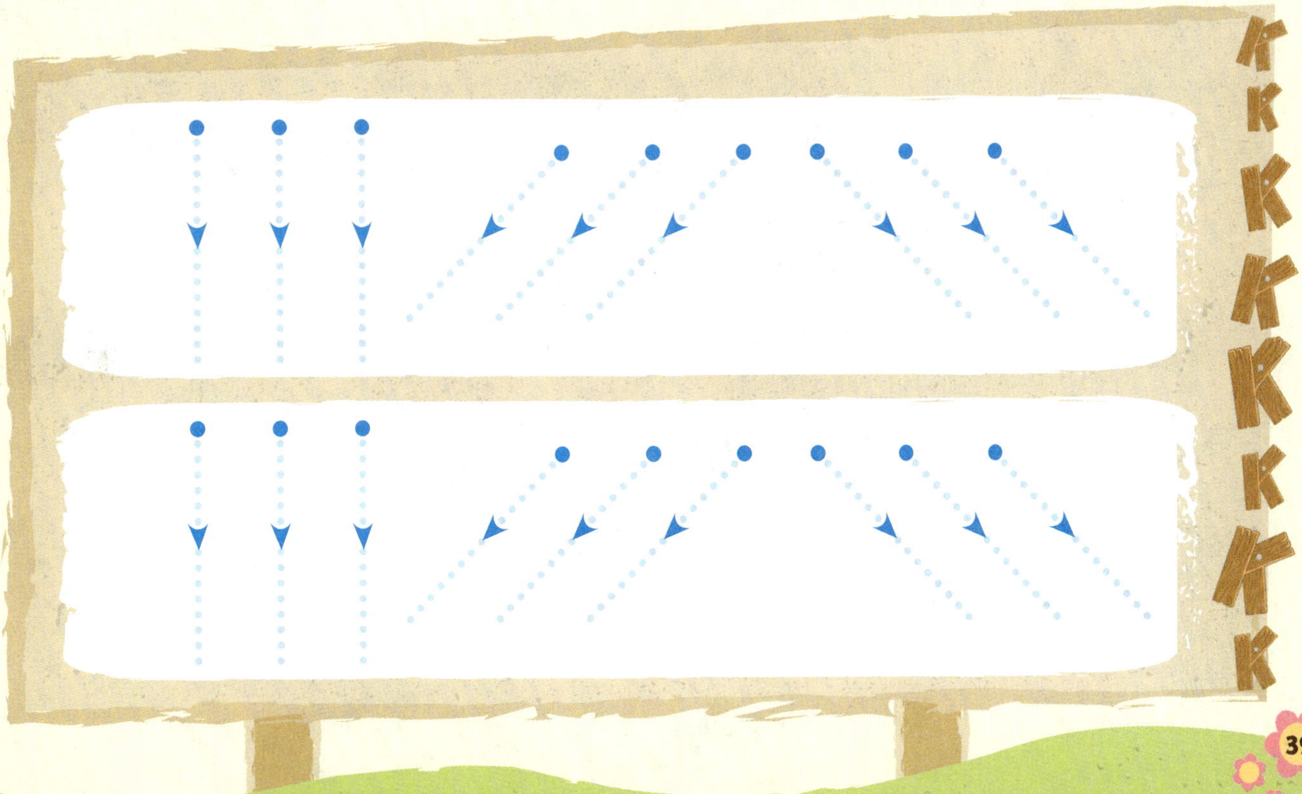

Hello Letter Ll

L l

lion

Touch the pictures. Name them.

lion

lollipop

lotus

lemon

leaf

Trace with your finger.

I Know Letters Ii-Ll

Colour the picture that begins with the given letter.

Ii

Jj

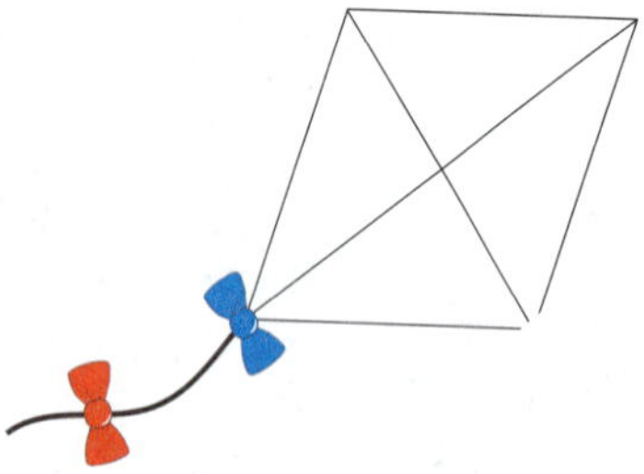

Kk

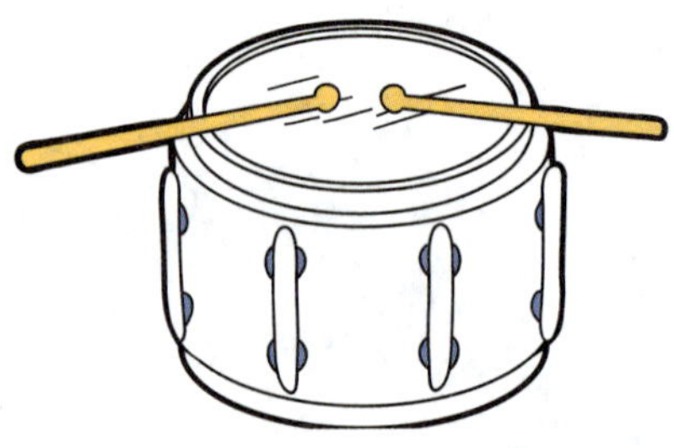

Ll

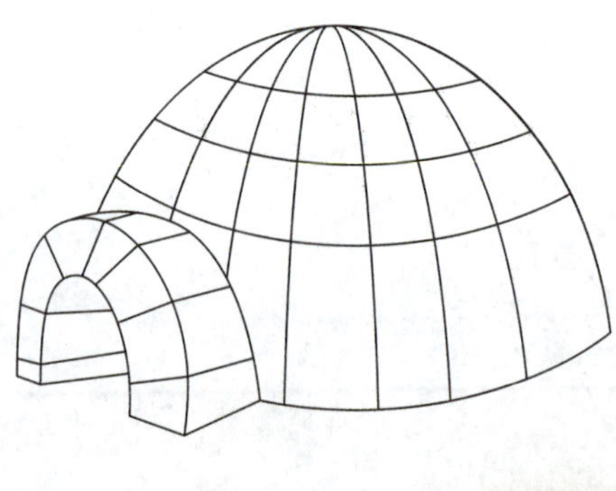

Match the picture to the letter it begins with.

Colour the matching letters in the same colour.

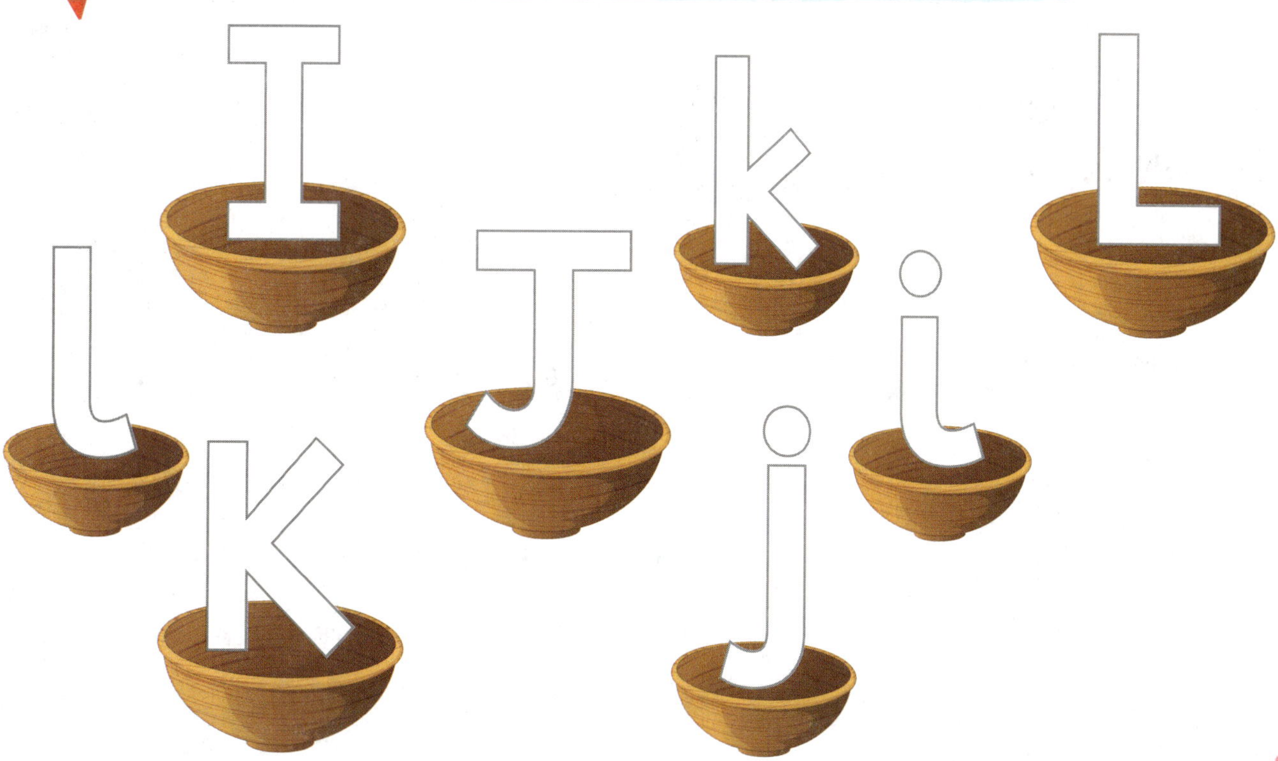

Play this game with your friends.

Teacher's Note:

Give children counters and dice to play this game. Initially, children may also toss a coin, moving forward only if they land a heads. This game can be played to reinforce letter-sound association and develop vocabulary.

Hello Letter Mm

Mm

monkey

Touch the pictures. Name them.

mat

monkey

mug

man

mango

Trace with your finger.

Hello Letter Nn

Nn

numbat

Touch the pictures. Name them.

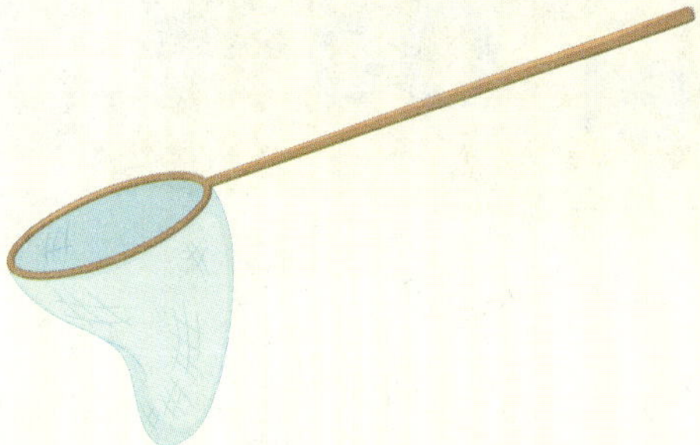

net

nuts

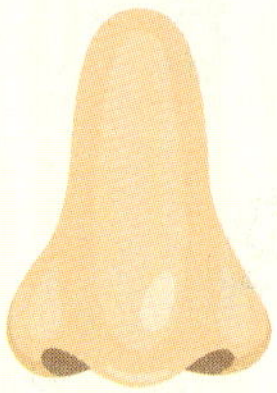

nose

nest

nine

Trace with your finger.

Hello Letter Oo

ostrich

Touch the pictures. Name them.

ox

octopus

ostrich

olive

orange

Trace with your finger.

Hello Letter Pp

Pp

panda

Touch the pictures. Name them.

pen

peacock

pin

parrot

pan

Trace with your finger.

I Know Letters Mm-Pp

Cross (×) the odd one out.

Mm

Nn

Oo

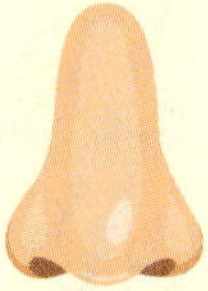

Pp

Paste matching letter stickers.

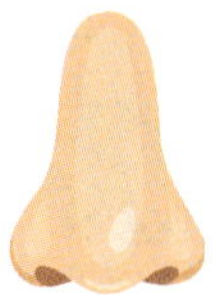

Listen and cross out (×).

Teacher's Note: Play bingo with your students.

Hello Letter Qq

Qq

quail

Touch the pictures. Name them.

quiet

quilt

quail

queen

quill

Trace with your finger.

Hello Letter Rr

rhinoceros

Touch the pictures. Name them.

rain

rainbow

rabbit

rose

rat

Trace with your finger.

Hello Letter Ss

Touch the pictures. Name them.

snail

snake

sun

soap

spoon

Trace with your finger.

Hello Letter Tt

Tt

tiger

Touch the pictures. Name them.

toy

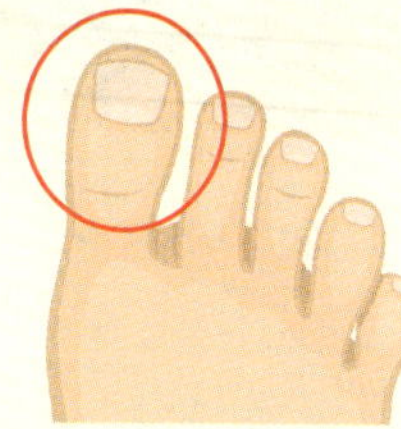

toe

tiger

tree

tub

Trace with your finger.

Hello Letter Uu

Uu

urn

Touch the pictures. Name them.

up

umbrella

urn

under

umpire

Trace with your finger.

I Know Letters Qq–Uu

Match the picture to the letter it begins with.

Ss

Uu

Tt

Rr

Qq

Paste small letters next to the capital letters on the web.

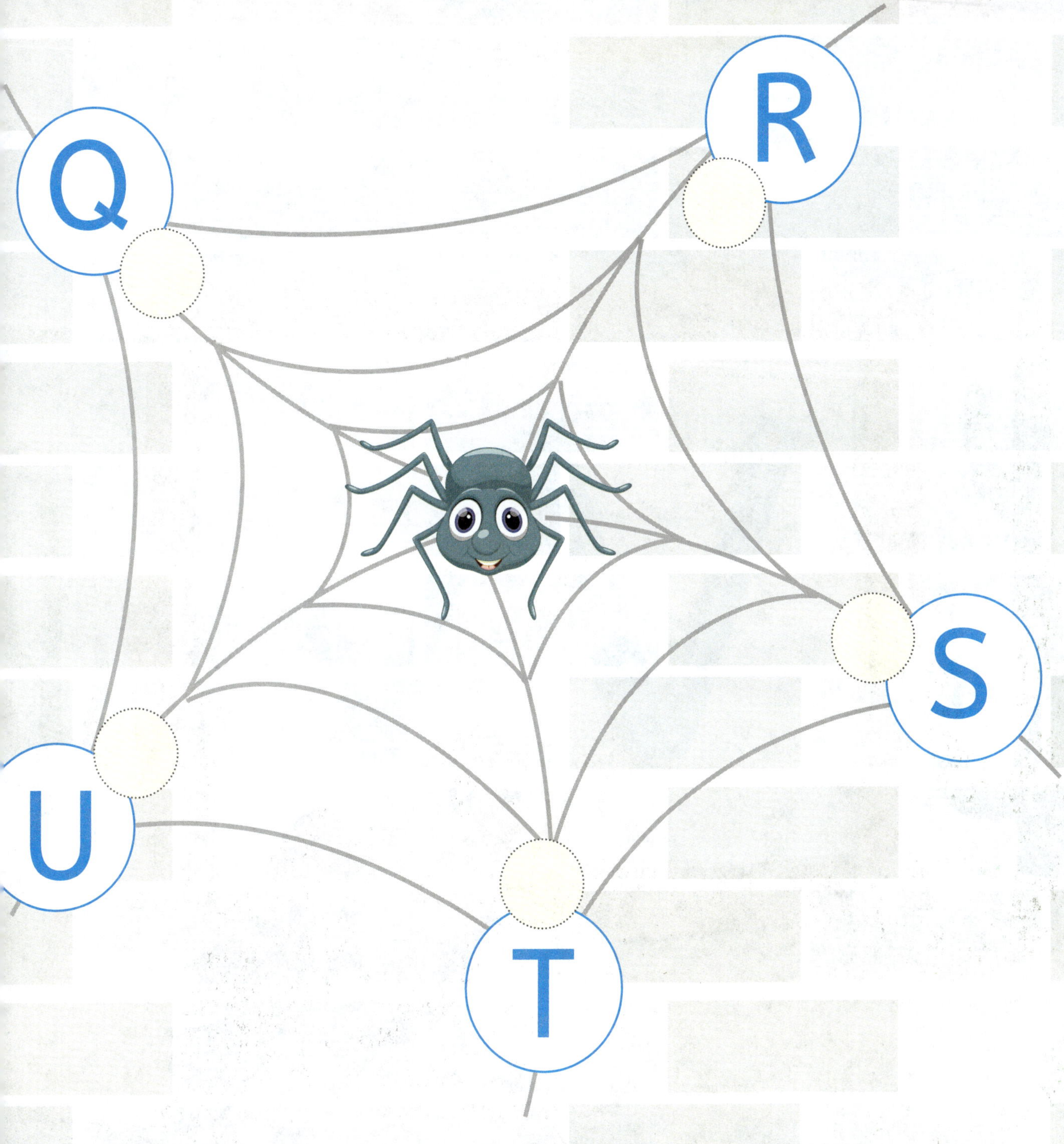

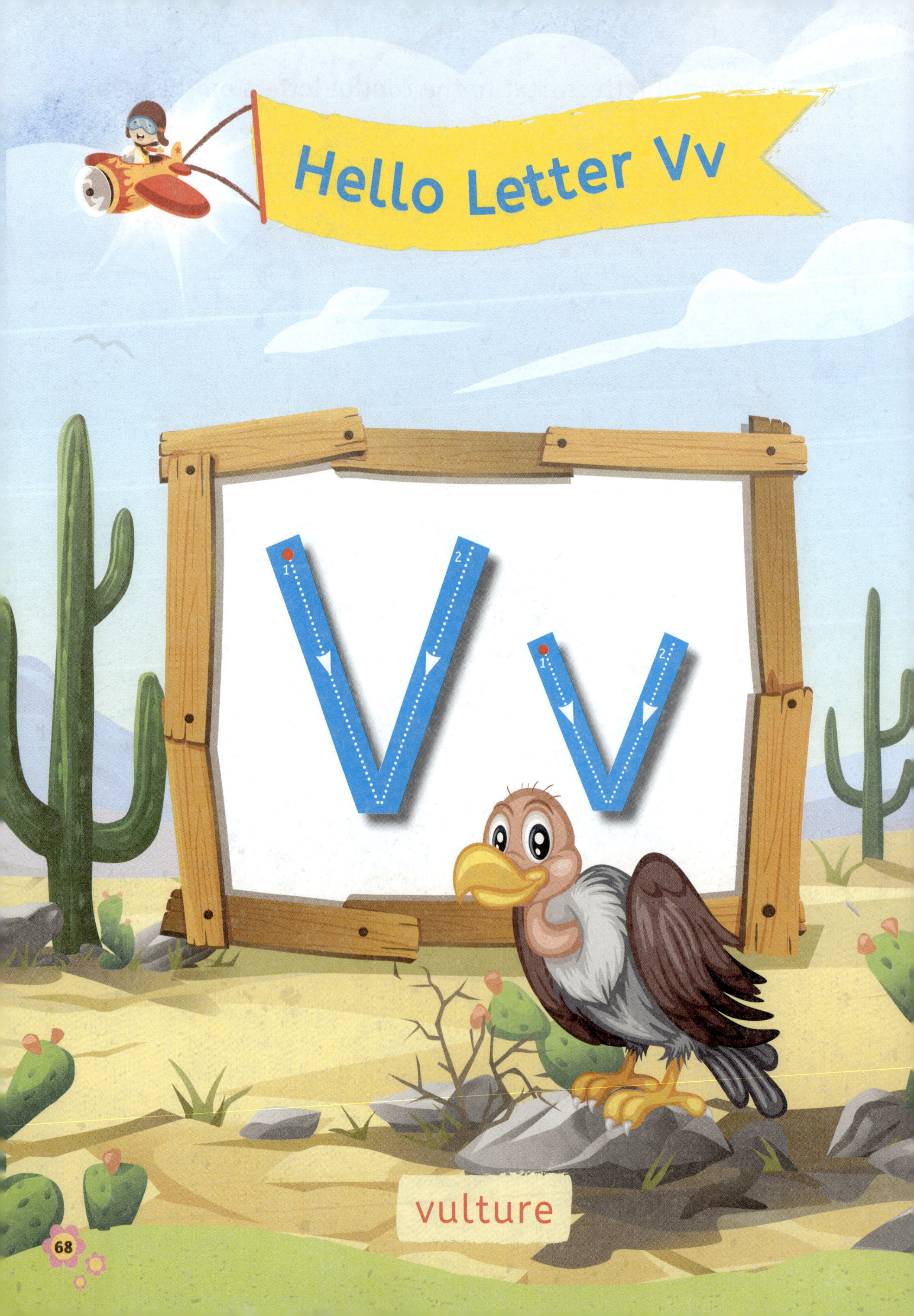
Hello Letter Vv
V v
vulture

Touch the pictures. Name them.

vulture

van

vegetables

vase

violin

Trace with your finger.

Hello Letter Ww

whale

Touch the pictures. Name them.

watch

window

watermelon

web

wolf

Trace with your finger.

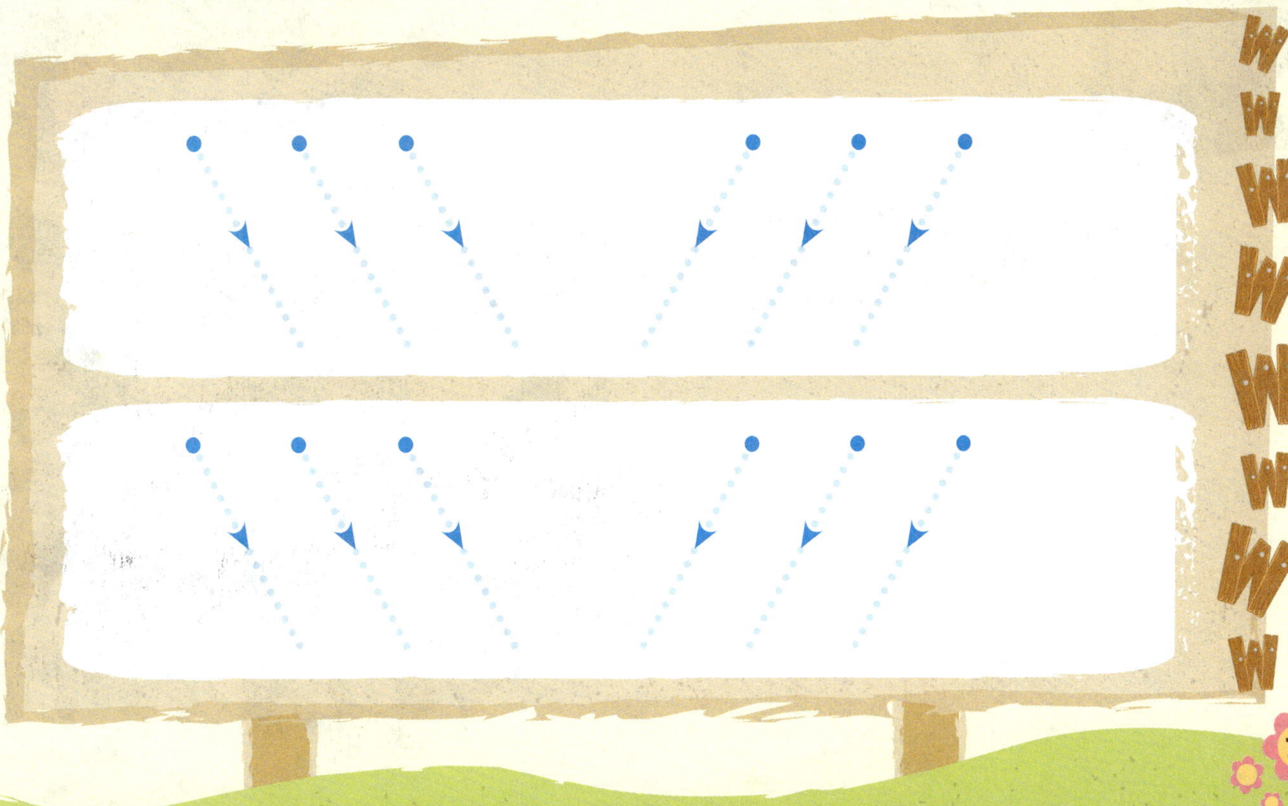

Hello Letter Xx
X x
x-mas tree

Touch the pictures. Name them.

fox

x-mas tree

box

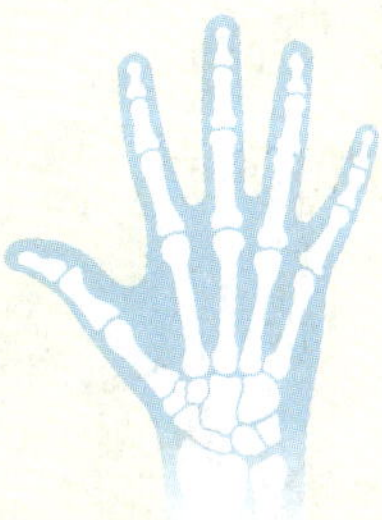

x-ray

six

Trace with your finger.

Hello Letter Yy

Touch the pictures. Name them.

yogurt

yak

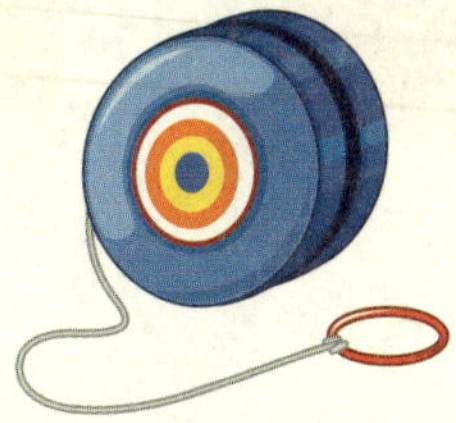

yo-yo

yacht

yarn

Trace with your finger.

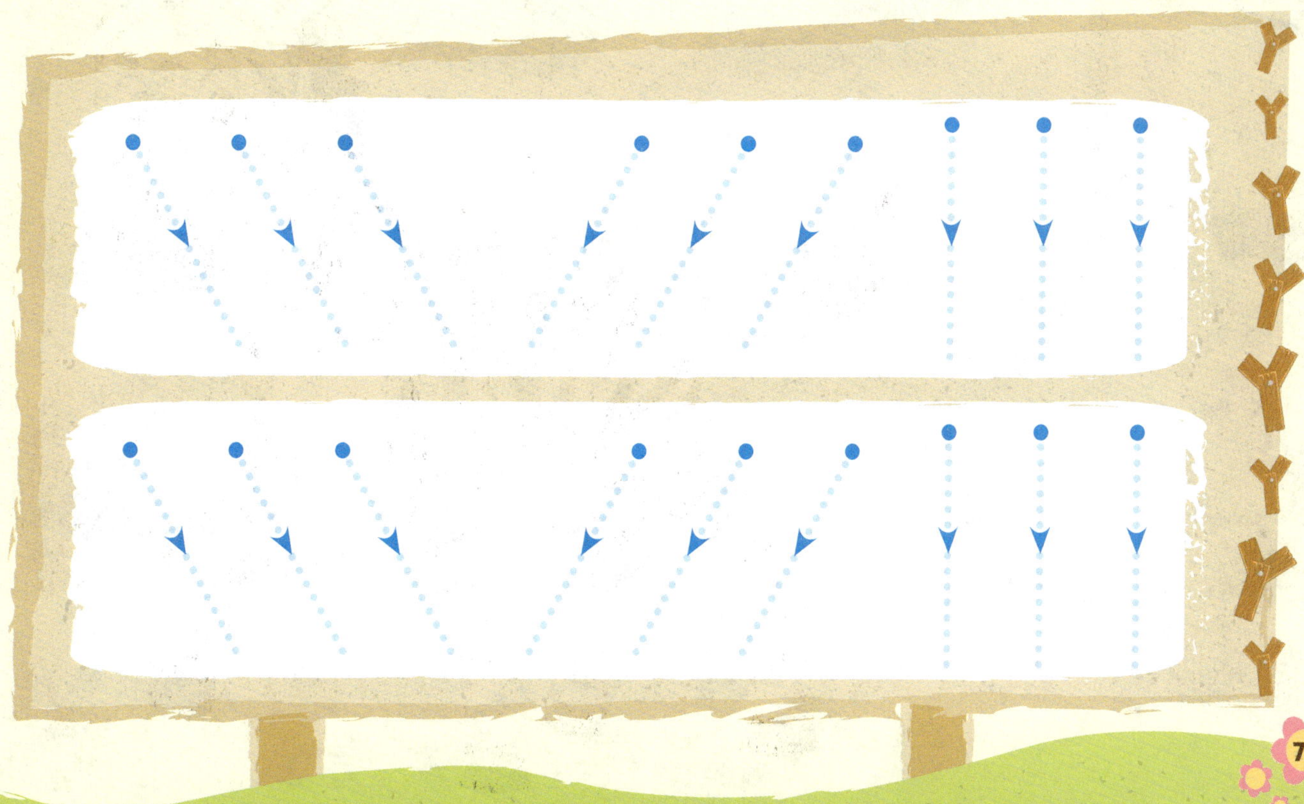

Hello Letter Zz

Z z

zebra

Touch the pictures. Name them.

zip

zebra

zoo

zig zag

zero

Trace with your finger.

I Know Letters Vv–Zz

Colour the pictures. Name them. Circle the letter they begin with.

Xx

Ww

Vv

Yy

Xx

Vv

Yy

Zz

Xx

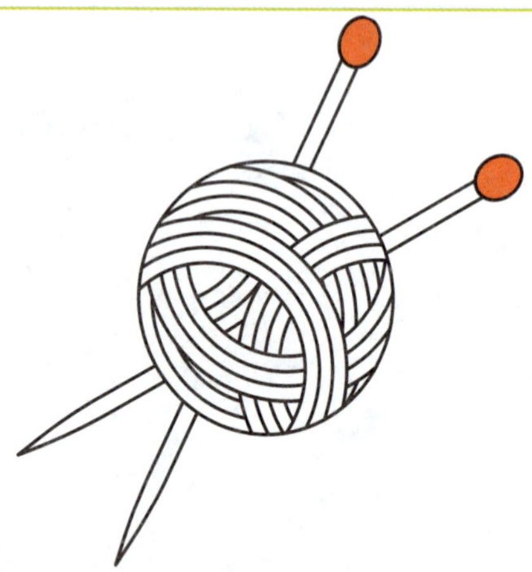

Zz

Yy

Vv

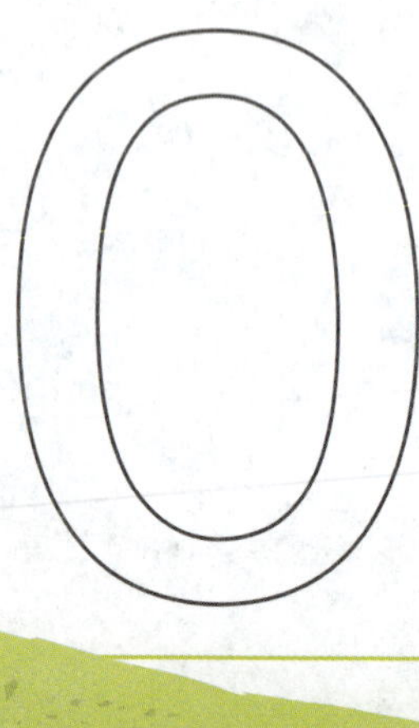

Yy

Zz

Xx

Match the pictures to the correct letters.

Mixed Revision Bag

Paste the letters from a-z to complete the caterpillar.

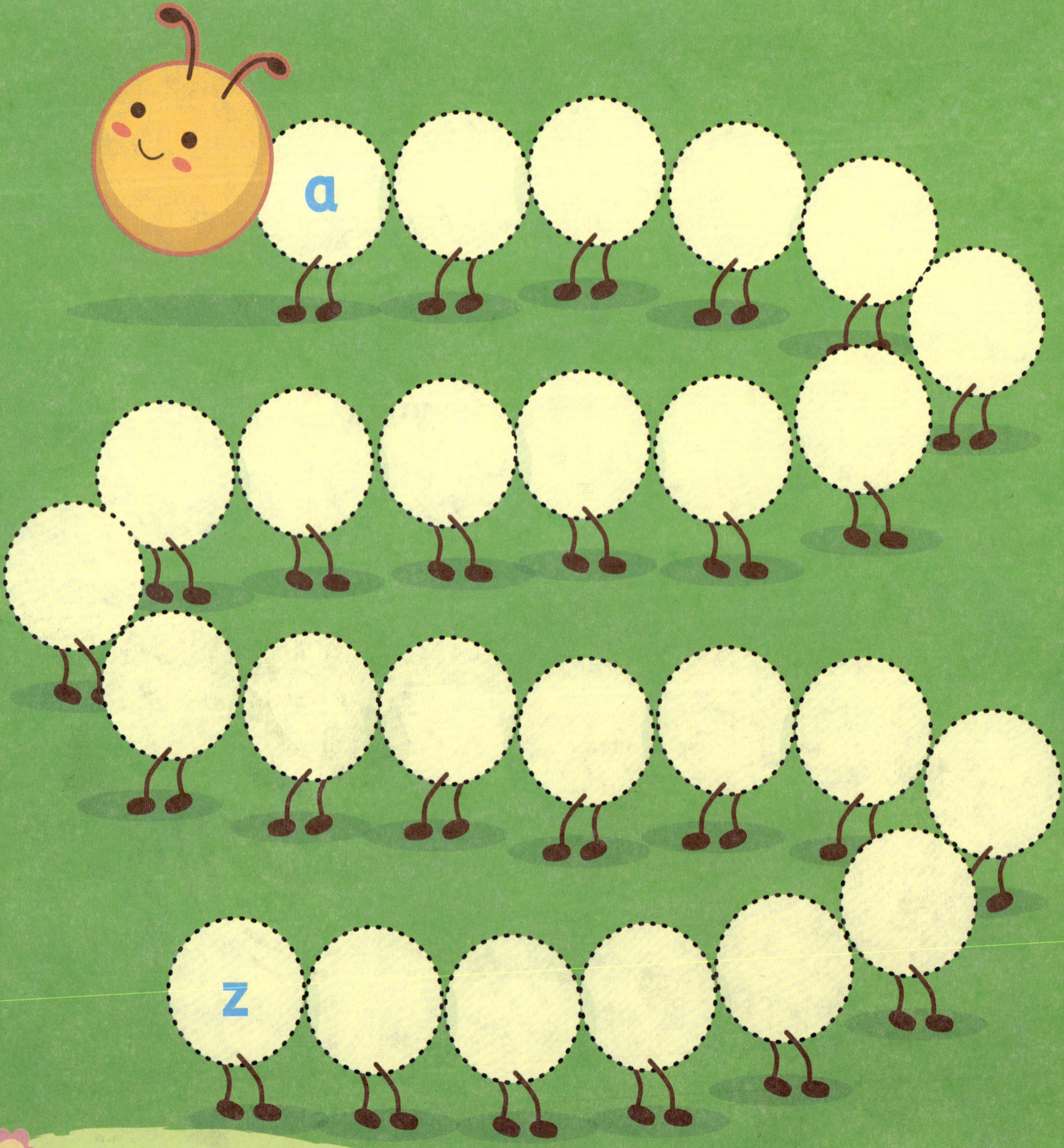

Sticker Page

E F G H

M N O P

q r s t u

a b c d e f g

h i j k l m n

o p q r s t u

v w x y z